The Ducks and the Tortoise

with

The Bear and the Travellers

Illustrated by Val Biro

Award Publications Limited

There once lived a tortoise who was tired of crawling.

"My legs are short and my shell is heavy," he sighed. "I wish I could fly. Then I could really see the world."

Two ducks heard the tortoise and landed nearby.

"You can't fly without wings," they told him. But the tortoise begged them to teach him.

At last they agreed.

"Hold this stick tightly in your mouth and we will take you flying," said the brown duck.

The ducks carried the
the tortoise high over
a village.

The villagers were amazed to see a tortoise up in the air. They waved and cheered.

The tortoise felt he must be very clever to be able to fly like that. He opened his mouth to shout, "Look at me! I can fly!"

As soon as he opened his mouth he let go of the stick and fell to earth with a bump.
He was not so clever after all!

The Bear and the Travellers

Two friends were travelling together on a lonely road. One of them was an old man and the other was younger.

They came to a deep, dark wood. "If we stick together we will come to no harm," said the old man.

The younger man agreed. Suddenly a huge brown bear came out of the bushes. It had sharp teeth and looked fierce.

"Here comes my dinner!" growled the bear. He licked his lips hungrily.

The two men ran away
and the bear chased after them.
The old man could not run as fast
as his younger friend.

The old man was sure the bear would catch him. He called to his friend, "Take my stick and fight the bear!"

But instead the younger man climbed a tree to escape from the bear.

It was said that a bear would not eat someone who was dead. So the old man pretended to be dead.

He closed his eyes and did not move.

His friend stayed in the tree.

The old man held his breath while the bear sniffed him from head to toe.

"I cannot reach the man in the tree, and this one is dead. I never eat dead people," the bear growled and walked away.

When at last the bear was out of sight, the younger man climbed down from the tree. He was amazed.

"The bear did not eat you, my friend!" he gasped. "I saw him whisper in your ear as he sniffed you. What did he say?"

The old man looked sternly at his friend who had not helped him when he was in danger.

"He told me that a true friend will never let you down."